Key Facts™ on

Australia

~Essential Information on Australia~

By Patrick W. Nee

The Internationalist®

www.internationalist.com

The Internationalist®

International Business, Investment, and Travel

Published by:

The Internationalist Publishing Company

96 Walter Street/ Suite 200

Boston, MA 02131, USA

Tel: 617-354-7722

www.internationalist.com

PN@internationalist.com

Table Of Contents

Chapter 1: Background

Chapter 2: Geography

Chapter 3: People and Society

Chapter 4: Government and Key Leaders

Chapter 5: Economy

Chapter 6: Energy

Chapter 7: Communications

Chapter 8: Transportation

Chapter 9: Military

Chapter 10: Transnational Issues

Map of Australia

Chapter 1: Background

Prehistoric settlers arrived on the continent from Southeast Asia at least 40,000 years before the first Europeans began exploration in the 17th century. No formal territorial claims were made until 1770, when Capt. James COOK took possession of the east coast in the name of Great Britain (all of Australia was claimed as British territory in 1829 with the creation of the colony of Western Australia). Six colonies were created in the late 18th and 19th centuries; they federated and became the Commonwealth of Australia in 1901. The new country took advantage of its natural resources to rapidly develop agricultural and manufacturing industries and to make a major contribution to the Allied effort in World Wars I and II. In recent decades, Australia has become an internationally competitive, advanced market economy due in large part to economic reforms adopted in the 1980s and its location in one of the fastest growing regions of the world economy. Long-term concerns include aging of the population, pressure on infrastructure, and environmental issues such as floods, droughts, and bushfires. Australia is the driest inhabited continent on earth, making it particularly vulnerable to the challenges of climate change. Australia is home to 10 per cent of the world's biodiversity, and a great number of its flora and fauna exist nowhere else in the world. In January 2013, Australia assumed a nonpermanent seat on the UN Security Council for the 2013-14 term.

Chapter 2: Geography

Location:

Oceania, continent between the Indian Ocean and the South Pacific Ocean

Geographic coordinates:

27 00 S, 133 00 E

Map references:

Oceania

Area:

total: 7,741,220 sq km

country comparison to the world: 6

land: 7,682,300 sq km

water: 58,920 sq km

note: includes Lord Howe Island and Macquarie Island

Area - comparative:

slightly smaller than the US contiguous 48 states

Land boundaries:

0 km

Coastline:

25,760 km

Maritime claims:

territorial sea: 12 nm

contiguous zone: 24 nm

exclusive economic zone: 200 nm

continental shelf: 200 nm or to the edge of the
continental margin

Climate:

generally arid to semiarid; temperate in south and
east; tropical in north

Terrain:

mostly low plateau with deserts; fertile plain in
southeast

Elevation extremes:

lowest point: Lake Eyre -15 m

highest point: Mount Kosciuszko 2,229 m

Natural resources:

bauxite, coal, iron ore, copper, tin, gold, silver,
uranium, nickel, tungsten, rare earth elements,
mineral sands, lead, zinc, diamonds, natural gas,
petroleum

note: Australia is the world's largest net exporter of
coal accounting for 29% of global coal exports

Land use:

arable land: 6.16% (includes about 27 million
hectares of cultivated grassland)

permanent crops: 0.05%

<u>other</u>: 93.79% (2011)

Irrigated land:

25,460 sq km (2006)

Total renewable water resources:

492 cu km (2011)

Freshwater withdrawal (domestic/industrial/agricultural):

<u>total</u>: 22.58 cu km/yr (27%/18%/55%)

<u>per capita</u>: 1,152 cu m/yr (2010)

Natural hazards:

cyclones along the coast; severe droughts; forest fires

<u>volcanism</u>: volcanic activity on Heard and McDonald Islands

Environment - current issues:

soil erosion from overgrazing, industrial development, urbanization, and poor farming practices; soil salinity rising due to the use of poor quality water; desertification; clearing for agricultural purposes threatens the natural habitat of many unique animal and plant species; the Great Barrier Reef off the northeast coast, the largest coral reef in the world, is threatened by increased shipping and its popularity as a tourist site; limited natural freshwater resources

Environment - international agreements:

party to: Antarctic-Environmental Protocol, Antarctic-Marine Living Resources, Antarctic Seals, Antarctic Treaty, Biodiversity, Climate Change, Climate Change-Kyoto Protocol, Desertification, Endangered Species, Environmental Modification, Hazardous Wastes, Law of the Sea, Marine Dumping, Marine Life Conservation, Ozone Layer Protection, Ship Pollution, Tropical Timber 83, Tropical Timber 94, Wetlands, Whaling

signed, but not ratified: none of the selected agreements

Geography - note:

world's smallest continent but sixth-largest country; the only continent without glaciers; population concentrated along the eastern and southeastern coasts; the invigorating sea breeze known as the "Fremantle Doctor" affects the city of Perth on the west coast and is one of the most consistent winds in the world

Chapter 3: People and Society

Nationality:

noun: Australian(s)

adjective: Australian

Ethnic groups:

white 92%, Asian 7%, aboriginal and other 1%

Languages:

English 78.5%, Chinese 2.5%, Italian 1.6%, Greek 1.3%, Arabic 1.2%, Vietnamese 1%, other 8.2%, unspecified 5.7% (2006 Census)

Religions:

Protestant 27.4% (Anglican 18.7%, Uniting Church 5.7%, Presbyterian and Reformed 3%), Catholic 25.8%, Eastern Orthodox 2.7%, other Christian 7.9%, Buddhist 2.1%, Muslim 1.7%, other 2.4%, unspecified 11.3%, none 18.7% (2006 Census)

Population:

22,262,501 (July 2013 est.)

country comparison to the world: 55

Age structure:

0-14 years: 18.1% (male 2,061,973/female 1,957,558)

15-24 years: 13.4% (male 1,531,325/female 1,453,940)

25-54 years: 42% (male 4,748,667/female 4,598,259)

55-64 years: 11.8% (male 1,308,660/female 1,326,220)

65 years and over: 14.7% (male 1,509,460/female 1,766,439) (2013 est.)

Median age:

total: 38.1 years

male: 37.3 years

female: 38.8 years (2013 est.)

Population growth rate:

1.11% (2013 est.)

country comparison to the world: 106

Birth rate:

12.23 births/1,000 population (2013 est.)

country comparison to the world: 162

Death rate:

7.01 deaths/1,000 population (2013 est.)

country comparison to the world: 132

Net migration rate:

5.83 migrant(s)/1,000 population (2013 est.)

country comparison to the world: 20

Urbanization:

urban population: 89% of total population (2010)

rate of urbanization: 1.2% annual rate of change (2010-15 est.)

Major urban areas - population:

Sydney 4.429 million; Melbourne 3.853 million; Brisbane 1.97 million; Perth 1.599 million; CANBERRA (capital) 399,000 (2011)

Sex ratio:

at birth: 1.06 male(s)/female

0-14 years: 1.05 male(s)/female

15-24 years: 1.05 male(s)/female

25-54 years: 1.03 male(s)/female

55-64 years: 0.99 male(s)/female

65 years and over: 0.85 male(s)/female

total population: 1.01 male(s)/female (2013 est.)

Maternal mortality rate:

7 deaths/100,000 live births (2010)

country comparison to the world: 166

Infant mortality rate:

total: 4.49 deaths/1,000 live births

country comparison to the world: 190

male: 4.8 deaths/1,000 live births

female: 4.15 deaths/1,000 live births (2013 est.)

Life expectancy at birth:

total population: 81.98 years

country comparison to the world: 10

male: 79.55 years

female: 84.54 years (2013 est.)

Total fertility rate:

1.77 children born/woman (2013 est.)

country comparison to the world: 162

Contraceptive prevalence rate:

72.3%

note: percent of women aged 18-44 (2005)

Health expenditures:

8.7% of GDP (2010)

country comparison to the world: 48

Physicians density:

2.99 physicians/1,000 population (2009)

Hospital bed density:

3.82 beds/1,000 population (2009)

Drinking water source:

improved:

urban: 100% of population

rural: 100% of population

total: 100% of population (2010 est.)

Sanitation facility access:

improved:

urban: 100% of population

rural: 100% of population

total: 100% of population (2010 est.)

HIV/AIDS - adult prevalence rate:

0.1% (2009 est.)

country comparison to the world: 110

HIV/AIDS - people living with HIV/AIDS:

20,000 (2009 est.)

country comparison to the world: 76

HIV/AIDS - deaths:

fewer than 100 (2009 est.)

country comparison to the world: 123

Obesity - adult prevalence rate:

26.8% (2008)

country comparison to the world: 44

Education expenditures:

5.1% of GDP (2009)

country comparison to the world: 71

Literacy:

definition: age 15 and over can read and write

total population: 99%

male: 99%

female: 99% (2003 est.)

School life expectancy (primary to tertiary education):

total: 20 years

<u>male</u>: 19 years

<u>female</u>: 20 years (2010)

Unemployment, youth ages 15-24:

<u>total</u>: 11.3%

<u>country comparison to the world</u>: 101

<u>male</u>: 11.9%

<u>female</u>: 10.8% (2011)

Mother's mean age at first birth:

30.5 (2006 est.)

Chapter 4: Government and Key Leaders

Country name:

conventional long form: Commonwealth of Australia

conventional short form: Australia

Government type:

federal parliamentary democracy and a
Commonwealth realm

Capital:

name: Canberra

geographic coordinates: 35 16 S, 149 08 E

time difference: UTC+10 (15 hours ahead of
Washington, DC during Standard Time)

daylight saving time: +1hr, begins first Sunday in
October; ends first Sunday in April

note: Australia is divided into three time zones

Administrative divisions:

6 states and 2 territories*; Australian Capital
Territory*, New South Wales, Northern Territory*,
Queensland, South Australia, Tasmania, Victoria,
Western Australia

Dependent areas:

Ashmore and Cartier Islands, Christmas Island, Cocos
(Keeling) Islands, Coral Sea Islands, Heard Island

and McDonald Islands, Macquarie Island, Norfolk
Island

Independence:

1 January 1901 (from the federation of UK colonies)

National holiday:

Australia Day (commemorates the arrival of the First
Fleet of Australian settlers), 26 January (1788);
ANZAC Day (commemorates the anniversary of the
landing of troops of the Australian and New Zealand
Army Corps during World War I at Gallipoli,
Turkey), 25 April (1915)

Constitution:

9 July 1900; effective 1 January 1901

Legal system:

common law system based on the English model

International law organization participation:

accepts compulsory ICJ jurisdiction with
reservations; accepts ICCt jurisdiction

Suffrage:

18 years of age; universal and compulsory

Executive branch:

chief of state: Queen of Australia ELIZABETH II
(since 6 February 1952); represented by Governor
General Quentin BRYCE (since 5 September 2008)

head of government: Prime Minister Kevin RUDD (since 27 June 2013); Deputy Prime Minister Anthony N. ALBANESE (since 27 June 2013)

cabinet: prime minister nominates, from among members of Parliament, candidates who are subsequently sworn in by the governor general to serve as government ministers

elections: the monarchy is hereditary; governor general appointed by the monarch on the recommendation of the prime minister; following legislative elections, the leader of the majority party or leader of a majority coalition is sworn in as prime minister by the governor general

Legislative branch:

bicameral Federal Parliament consists of the Senate (76 seats; 12 members from each of the six states and 2 from each of the two mainland territories; one-half of state members are elected every three years by popular vote to serve six-year terms while all territory members are elected every three years) and the House of Representatives (150 seats; members elected by popular vote to serve terms of up to three-years; no state can have fewer than 5 representatives) elections: Senate - last held on 21 August 2010; House of Representatives - last held on 21 August 2010 (the latest a simultaneous half-Senate and House of Representative elections can be held is 30 November 2013)

election results: Senate (effective 1 July 2011) - percent of vote by party - NA; seats by party - Liberal/National Coalition 34, Australian Labor Party 31, Australian Greens Party 9, others 2; House of Representatives - percent of vote by party - Australian Labor Party 38.1%, Liberal Party 30.4%, Australian Greens Party 11.5%, Liberal National Party of Queensland 9.3%, independents 6.6%, National Party of Australia 3.7%, Country Liberals 0.3%; seats by party - Australian Labor Party 72, Liberal Party 44, Liberal National Party of Queensland 21, National Party of Australia 7, Country Liberals 1, Australian Greens Party 1, independents 4

Judicial branch:

highest court(s): High Court of Australia (consists of 7 justices, including the chief justice); note - each of the 6 states, 2 territories, and Norfolk Island has a Supreme Court; the High Court is the final appellate court beyond the state and territory supreme courts judge selection and term of office: justices appointed by the governor-general in council for life with mandatory retirement at age 70

subordinate courts: subordinate courts at the federal level: Federal Court; Federal Magistrates' Courts of Australia; Family Court; subordinate courts at the state and territory level: Local Court - New South Wales; Magistrates' Courts – Victoria, Queensland, South Australia, Western Australia, Tasmania, Northern Territory, Australian Capital Territory; District Courts – New South Wales, Queensland, South Australia, Western Australia; County Court – Victoria; Family Court – Western Australia; Court of Petty Sessions – Norfolk Island

Political parties and leaders:

Australian Greens Party [Christine MILNE]

Australian Labor Party [Kevin RUDD]

Country Liberal Party [Terry MILLS]

Family First Party [Steve FIELDING]

Liberal National Party of Queensland [Campbell NEWMAN]

Liberal Party [Tony ABBOTT]

National Party of Australia [Warren TRUSS]

Political pressure groups and leaders:

<u>other</u>: business groups, environmental groups, social groups, trade unions

International organization participation:

ADB, ANZUS, APEC, ARF, ASEAN (dialogue partner), Australia Group, BIS, C, CD, CP, EAS, EBRD, EITI (implementing country), FAO, FATF, G-20, IAEA, IBRD, ICAO, ICC (national committees), ICRM, IDA, IEA, IFC, IFRCS, IHO, ILO, IMF, IMO, IMSO, Interpol, IOC, IOM, IPU, ISO, ITSO, ITU, ITUC (NGOs), MIGA, NEA, NSG, OECD, OPCW, OSCE (partner), Paris Club, PCA, PIF, SAARC (observer), SICA (observer), Sparteca, SPC, UN, UN Security Council (temporary), UNCTAD, UNESCO, UNHCR, UNMISS, UNMIT, UNRWA, UNTSO, UNWTO, UPU, WCO, WFTU (NGOs), WHO, WIPO, WMO, WTO, ZC

Diplomatic representation in the US:

<u>chief of mission</u>: Ambassador Kim Christian BEAZLEY

<u>chancery</u>: 1601 Massachusetts Avenue NW, Washington, DC 20036

<u>telephone</u>: [1] (202) 797-3000

<u>FAX</u>: [1] (202) 797-3168

consulate(s) general: Atlanta, Chicago, Honolulu, Los Angeles, New York, San Francisco

Diplomatic representation from the US:

chief of mission: Ambassador Jeffrey L. BLEICH

embassy: Moonah Place, Yarralumla, Canberra, Australian Capital Territory 2600

mailing address: APO AP 96549

telephone: [61] (02) 6214-5600

FAX: [61] (02) 6214-5970

consulate(s) general: Melbourne, Perth, Sydney

Key Leaders:

Governor Gen.	Quentin Alice Louise BRYCE
Prime Min.	Kevin Michael RUDD
Dep. Prime Min.	Anthony Norman ALBANESE
Min. for Agriculture, Fisheries, & Forestry	Joel Andrew FITZGIBBON
Min. for the Arts	Anthony Stephen "Tony" BURKE
Min. for Broadband, Communications, & the Digital Economy	Anthony Norman ALBANESE
Min. for Climate Change	Mark Christopher BUTLER

Min. for Community Services	Julie Maree COLLINS
Min. for Competition Policy & Consumer Affairs	David John BRADBURY
Min. for Defense	Stephen Francis SMITH
Min. for Defense Materiel	Michael Joseph KELLY
Min. for Defense Science & Personnel	Warren Edward SNOWDON
Min. for Disability Reform	Jennifer Louise MACKLIN
Min. for Early Childhood, Childcare, & Youth	Katherine Margaret ELLIS
Min. for Education	William Richard SHORTEN
Min. for Emergency Management	Mark Alfred DREYFUS
Min. for Employment	Brendan Patrick John O'CONNOR
Min. for Employment Participation	Katherine Margaret ELLIS
Min. for the Environment, Heritage, & Water	Mark Christopher BUTLER
Min. for Families,	Jennifer Louise MACKLIN

Community Services, & Indigenous Affairs	
Min. for Finance & Deregulation	Penelope "Penny" Yingyen WONG
Min. for Foreign Affairs	Robert John CARR
Min. for Health & Medical Research	Tanya Joan PLIBERSEK
Min. for Higher Education	Kim John CARR
Min. for Home Affairs	Jason Dean CLARE
Min. for Housing & Homelessness	Julie Maree COLLINS
Min. for Human Services	Jan MCLUCAS
Min. for Immigration, Multicultural Affairs, & Citizenship	Anthony Stephen "Tony" BURKE
Min. for Indigenous Employment & Economic Development	Julie Maree COLLINS
Min. for Indigenous Health	Warren Edward SNOWDON
Min. for Infrastructure & Transport	Anthony Norman ALBANESE

Min. for Innovation, Industry, Science, & Research	Kim John CARR
Min. for Intl. Development	Melissa PARKE
Min. for Justice	Jason Dean CLARE
Min. for Mental Health & Aging	Jacinta COLLINS
Min. for Multicultural Affairs	Kate Alexander LUNDY
Min. for the Public Service & Integrity	Mark Alfred DREYFUS
Min. for Regional Australia, Local Govt., & Territories	Catherine Fiona KING
Min. for Regional Communications	Sharon Leah BIRD
Min. for Regional Development	Sharon Leah BIRD
Min. for Resources & Energy	Gary GRAY
Min. for Road Safety	Sharon Leah BIRD
Min. for Skills & Training	Brendan Patrick John O'CONNOR

Min. for Small Business	Gary GRAY
Min. for Sport	Donald FARRELL
Min. for the Status of Women	Julie Maree COLLINS
Min. for Tourism	Gary GRAY
Min. for Trade	Richard Donald MARLES
Min. for Veterans Affairs	Warren Edward SNOWDON
Min. for Workplace Relations	William Richard SHORTEN
Treasurer	Chris Eyles BOWEN
Asst. Treasurer	David John BRADBURY
Min. Assisting the Prime Min. on the Centenary of ANZAC	Warren Edward SNOWDON
Min. Assisting for Deregulation	David John BRADBURY
Min. Assisting for the Digital Economy	Kate Alexander LUNDY
Min. Assisting for Financial Services & Superannuation	David John BRADBURY
Min. Assisting for	Kate Alexander LUNDY

Innovation & Industry	
Min. Assisting on Tourism	Donald FARRELL
Special Min. of State	Mark Alfred DREYFUS
Cabinet Sec.	Alan Peter GRIFFIN
Attorney Gen.	Mark Alfred DREYFUS
Governor, Reserve Bank of Australia	Glenn Robert STEVENS
Ambassador to the US	Kim Christian BEAZLEY
Permanent Representative to the UN, New York	Gary Francis QUINLAN

Flag description:

blue with the flag of the UK in the upper hoist-side quadrant and a large seven-pointed star in the lower hoist-side quadrant known as the Commonwealth or Federation Star, representing the federation of the colonies of Australia in 1901; the star depicts one point for each of the six original states and one representing all of Australia's internal and external territories; on the fly half is a representation of the Southern Cross constellation in white with one small, five-pointed star and four larger, seven-pointed stars

National symbol(s):

Southern Cross constellation (five, seven-pointed stars); kangaroo; emu

National anthem:

name: "Advance Australia Fair"

lyrics/music: Peter Dodds McCORMICK

note: adopted 1984; although originally written in the late 19th century, the anthem did not become used for all official occasions until 1984; as a Commonwealth country, in addition to the national anthem, "God Save the Queen" is also played at Royal functions

Chapter 5: Economy

Economy - overview:

The Australian economy has experienced continuous growth and features low unemployment, contained inflation, very low public debt, and a strong and stable financial system. By 2012, Australia had experienced more than 20 years of continued economic growth, averaging 3.5% a year. Demand for resources and energy from Asia and especially China has grown rapidly, creating a channel for resources investments and growth in commodity exports. The high Australian dollar has hurt the manufacturing sector, while the services sector is the largest part of the Australian economy, accounting for about 70% of GDP and 75% of jobs. Australia was comparatively unaffected by the global financial crisis as the banking system has remained strong and inflation is under control. Australia has benefited from a dramatic surge in its terms of trade in recent years, stemming from rising global commodity prices. Australia is a significant exporter of natural resources, energy, and food. Australia's abundant and diverse natural resources attract high levels of foreign investment and include extensive reserves of coal, iron, copper, gold, natural gas, uranium, and renewable energy sources. A series of major investments, such as the US$40 billion Gorgon Liquid Natural Gas project, will significantly expand the resources sector. Australia is an open market with minimal restrictions on imports of goods and services. The process of opening up has increased productivity, stimulated growth, and made the economy more flexible and dynamic. Australia plays an active role in the World Trade Organization, APEC, the G20, and other trade forums. Australia has bilateral free trade agreements (FTAs) with Chile, Malaysia, New Zealand, Singapore, Thailand, and the US, has a regional FTA with ASEAN and New Zealand, is negotiating agreements with China, India, Indonesia, Japan, and the Republic of Korea, as well as with its Pacific neighbors and the Gulf Cooperation Council countries, and is also working on the Trans-Pacific Partnership Agreement with Brunei Darussalam, Canada, Chile, Malaysia, Mexico, New Zealand, Peru, Singapore, the US, and Vietnam.

GDP (purchasing power parity):

$986.7 billion (2012 est.)

country comparison to the world: 19

$952.6 billion (2011 est.)

$930 billion (2010 est.)

note: data are in 2012 US dollars

GDP (official exchange rate):

$1.542 trillion (2012 est.)

GDP - real growth rate:

3.6% (2012 est.)

country comparison to the world: 94

2.4% (2011 est.)

2.6% (2010 est.)

GDP - per capita (PPP):

$43,300 (2012 est.)

country comparison to the world: 20

$42,400 (2011 est.)

$41,900 (2010 est.)

note: data are in 2012 US dollars

GDP - composition by sector:

agriculture: 4%

industry: 27.3%

services: 68.8% (2012 est.)

Labor force:

12.15 million (2012 est.)

country comparison to the world: 44

Labor force - by occupation:

agriculture: 3.6%

industry: 21.1%

services: 75% (2009 est.)

Unemployment rate:

5.2% (2012 est.)

country comparison to the world: 47

5.1% (2011 est.)

Household income or consumption by percentage share:

lowest 10%: 2%

highest 10%: 25.4% (1994)

Distribution of family income - Gini index:

30.3 (2008)

country comparison to the world: 114

35.2 (1994)

Investment (gross fixed):

28.5% of GDP (2012 est.)

country comparison to the world: 30

Budget:

revenues: $498.1 billion

expenditures: $541 billion (2012 est.)

Taxes and other revenues:

32.3% of GDP (2012 est.)

country comparison to the world: 79

Budget surplus (+) or deficit (-):

-2.8% of GDP (2012 est.)

country comparison to the world: 110

Public debt:

29.3% of GDP (2012 est.)

country comparison to the world: 118

26.6% of GDP (2011 est.)

Inflation rate (consumer prices):

1.8% (2012 est.)

country comparison to the world: 36

3.3% (2011 est.)

Central bank discount rate:

3% (February 2013 est.)

country comparison to the world: 82

4.35% (31 December 2010 est.)

note: this is the Reserve Bank of Australia's "cash rate target," or policy rate

Commercial bank prime lending rate:

6.98% (31 December 2012 est.)

country comparison to the world: 118

7.74% (31 December 2011 est.)

Stock of narrow money:

$534.8 billion (31 December 2012 est.)

country comparison to the world: 10

$475.9 billion (31 December 2011 est.)

Stock of broad money:

$1.708 trillion (31 December 2012 est.)

country comparison to the world: 11

$1.501 trillion (31 December 2011 est.)

Stock of domestic credit:

$2.255 trillion (31 December 2012 est.)

country comparison to the world: 12

$2.061 trillion (31 December 2011 est.)

Market value of publicly traded shares:

$1.4 trillion (31 January 2013)

country comparison to the world: 13

$1.198 trillion (31 December 2011)

$1.455 trillion (31 December 2010)

Agriculture - products:

wheat, barley, sugarcane, fruits; cattle, sheep, poultry

Industries:

mining, industrial and transportation equipment, food processing, chemicals, steel

Industrial production growth rate:

3.6% (2012 est.)

country comparison to the world: 77

Current account balance:

-$47.1 billion (2012 est.)

country comparison to the world: 186

-$29.5 billion (2011 est.)

Exports:

$258.8 billion (2012 est.)

<u>country comparison to the world</u>: 23

$271.6 billion (2011 est.)

Exports - commodities:

coal, iron ore, gold, meat, wool, alumina, wheat, machinery and transport equipment

Exports - partners:

China 29.5%, Japan 19.3%, South Korea 8%, India 4.9% (2012)

Imports:

$239.7 billion (2012 est.)

<u>country comparison to the world</u>: 21

$242.3 billion (2011 est.)

Imports - commodities:

machinery and transport equipment, computers and office machines, telecommunication equipment and parts; crude oil and petroleum products

Imports - partners:

China 18.2%, US 11.6%, Japan 7.8%, Singapore 5.9%, Germany 4.6%, Thailand 4.2%, South Korea 4% (2012)

Reserves of foreign exchange and gold:

$49.22 billion (31 December 2012 est.)

country comparison to the world: 39

$46.83 billion (31 December 2011 est.)

Debt - external:

$1.497 trillion (31 December 2012 est.)

country comparison to the world: 13

$1.383 trillion (31 December 2011 est.)

Stock of direct foreign investment - at home:

$618.9 billion (31 December 2012 est.)

country comparison to the world: 11

$552.8 billion (31 December 2011 est.)

Stock of direct foreign investment - abroad:

$426.5 billion (31 December 2012 est.)

country comparison to the world: 15

$378.7 billion (31 December 2011 est.)

Exchange rates:

Australian dollars (AUD) per US dollar -

0.9658 (2012 est.)

0.9695 (2011 est.)

1.0902 (2010)

1.2822 (2009)

1.2059 (2008)

Fiscal year:

1 July - 30 June

Chapter 6: Energy

Electricity - production:

> 241.5 billion kWh (2010 est.)

> country comparison to the world: 19

Electricity - consumption:

> 228.8 billion kWh (2009 est.)

> country comparison to the world: 18

Electricity - exports:

> 0 kWh (2010 est.)

> country comparison to the world: 158

Electricity - imports:

> 0 kWh (2010 est.)

> country comparison to the world: 157

Electricity - installed generating capacity:

> 56.94 million kW (2009 est.)

> country comparison to the world: 16

Electricity - from fossil fuels:

> 79% of total installed capacity (2009 est.)

> country comparison to the world: 95

Electricity - from nuclear fuels:

> 0% of total installed capacity (2009 est.)

> country comparison to the world: 42

Electricity - from hydroelectric plants:

13.7% of total installed capacity (2009 est.)

country comparison to the world: 108

Electricity - from other renewable sources:

4.7% of total installed capacity (2009 est.)

country comparison to the world: 41

Crude oil - production:

482,500 bbl/day (2011 est.)

country comparison to the world: 32

Crude oil - exports:

250,000 bbl/day (2009 est.)

country comparison to the world: 29

Crude oil - imports:

380,900 bbl/day (2009 est.)

country comparison to the world: 23

Crude oil - proved reserves:

1.426 billion bbl (1 January 2012 est.)

country comparison to the world: 38

Refined petroleum products - production:

674,700 bbl/day (2009 est.)

country comparison to the world: 27

Refined petroleum products - consumption:

1.023 million bbl/day (2011 est.)

country comparison to the world: 21

Refined petroleum products - exports:

64,730 bbl/day (2009 est.)

country comparison to the world: 53

Refined petroleum products - imports:

332,900 bbl/day (2009 est.)

country comparison to the world: 20

Natural gas - production:

44.99 billion cu m (2011 est.)

country comparison to the world: 23

Natural gas - consumption:

27.56 billion cu m (2011 est.)

country comparison to the world: 31

Natural gas - exports:

25.53 billion cu m (2011 est.)

country comparison to the world: 14

Natural gas - imports:

8.102 billion cu m (2011 est.)

country comparison to the world: 30

Natural gas - proved reserves:

788.6 billion cu m (1 January 2012 est.)

country comparison to the world: 29

Carbon dioxide emissions from consumption of energy:

405.3 million Mt (2010 est.)

country comparison to the world: 17

Chapter 7: Communications

Telephones - main lines in use:

10.57 million (2011)

country comparison to the world: 20

Telephones - mobile cellular:

24.49 million (2011)

country comparison to the world: 43

Telephone system:

general assessment: excellent domestic and

international service

domestic: domestic satellite system; significant use of

radiotelephone in areas of low population density;

rapid growth of mobile telephones

international: country code - 61; landing point for the

SEA-ME-WE-3 optical telecommunications

submarine cable with links to Asia, the Middle East,

and Europe; the Southern Cross fiber optic submarine

cable provides links to New Zealand and the United

States; satellite earth stations - 10 Intelsat (4 Indian

Ocean and 6 Pacific Ocean), 2 Inmarsat, 2 Globalstar,

5 other) (2007)

Broadcast media:

the Australian Broadcasting Corporation (ABC) runs multiple national and local radio networks and TV stations, as well as Australia Network, a TV service that broadcasts throughout the Asia-Pacific region and is the main public broadcaster; Special Broadcasting Service (SBS), a second large public broadcaster, operates radio and TV networks broadcasting in multiple languages; several large national commercial TV networks, a large number of local commercial TV stations, and hundreds of commercial radio stations are accessible; cable and satellite systems are available (2008)

Internet country code:

.au

Internet hosts:

17.081 million (2012)

country comparison to the world: 8

Internet users:

15.81 million (2009)

country comparison to the world: 25

Chapter 8: Transportation

Airports:

> 467 (2012)
>
> country comparison to the world: 18

Airports - with paved runways:

> total: 333
>
> over 3,047 m: 11
>
> 2,438 to 3,047 m: 13
>
> 1,524 to 2,437 m: 146
>
> 914 to 1,523 m: 149
>
> under 914 m: 14 (2012)

Airports - with unpaved runways:

> total: 134
>
> 1,524 to 2,437 m: 19
>
> 914 to 1,523 m: 101
>
> under 914 m: 14 (2012)

Heliports:

> 1 (2012)

Pipelines:

> condensate/gas 637 km; gas 30,054 km; liquid
> petroleum gas 240 km; oil 3,609 km; oil/gas/water
> 110 km; refined products 72 km (2013)

Railways:

total: 38,445 km

country comparison to the world: 7

broad gauge: 3,355 km 1.600-m gauge

standard gauge: 21,674 km 1.435-m gauge (650 km electrified)

narrow gauge: 9,539 km 1.067-m gauge (2,067 km electrified); 3,877 km 1.000-m gauge (2008)

Roadways:

total: 823,217 km

country comparison to the world: 9

paved: 356,343 km

unpaved: 466,874 km (2011)

Waterways:

2,000 km (mainly used for recreation on Murray and Murray-Darling river systems) (2011)

country comparison to the world: 43

Merchant marine:

total: 41

country comparison to the world: 75

by type: bulk carrier 8, cargo 7, liquefied gas 4, passenger 6, passenger/cargo 6, petroleum tanker 5, roll on/roll off 5

foreign-owned: 17 (Canada 5, Germany 2, Singapore 2, South Africa 1, UK 5, US 2) registered in other countries: 25 (Bahamas 1, Dominica 1, Fiji 2, Liberia 1, Netherlands 1, Panama 4, Singapore 12, Tonga 1, UK 1, US 1) (2010)

Ports and terminals:

Brisbane, Cairns, Dampier, Darwin, Fremantle, Gladstone, Geelong, Hay Point, Hobart, Jervis Bay, Melbourne, Newcastle, Port Adelaide, Port Dalrymple, Port Hedland, Port Kembla, Port Lincoln, Port Walcott, Sydney

Chapter 9: Military

Military branches:

> Australian Defense Force (ADF): Australian Army (includes Special Operations Command), Royal Australian Navy (includes Naval Aviation Force), Royal Australian Air Force, Joint Operations Command (JOC) (2013)

Military service age and obligation:

> 17 years of age for voluntary military service (with parental consent); no conscription; women allowed to serve in most combat roles, except the Army special forces (2013)

Manpower available for military service:

> males age 16-49: 5,316,464
>
> females age 16-49: 5,116,722 (2010 est.)

Manpower fit for military service:

> males age 16-49: 4,411,958
>
> females age 16-49: 4,239,985 (2010 est.)

Manpower reaching militarily significant age annually:

> male: 143,565
>
> female: 135,800 (2010 est.)

Military expenditures:

> 3% of GDP (2012)

<u>country comparison to the world</u>: 41

Chapter 10: Transnational Issues

Disputes - international:

In 2007, Australia and Timor-Leste agreed to a 50-year development zone and revenue sharing arrangement and deferred a maritime boundary; Australia asserts land and maritime claims to Antarctica; Australia's 2004 submission to the Commission on the Limits of the Continental Shelf (CLCS) extends its continental margins over 3.37 million square kilometers, expanding its seabed roughly 30 percent beyond its claimed exclusive economic zone; all borders between Indonesia and Australia have been agreed upon bilaterally, but a 1997 treaty that would settle the last of their maritime and Exclusive Economic Zone (EEZ) boundary has yet to be ratified by Indonesia's legislature; Indonesian groups challenge Australia's claim to Ashmore Reef; Australia closed parts of the Ashmore and Cartier reserve to Indonesian traditional fishing

Illicit drugs:

Tasmania is one of the world's major suppliers of licit opiate products; government maintains strict controls over areas of opium poppy cultivation and output of poppy straw concentrate; major consumer of cocaine and amphetamines

Map of Australia

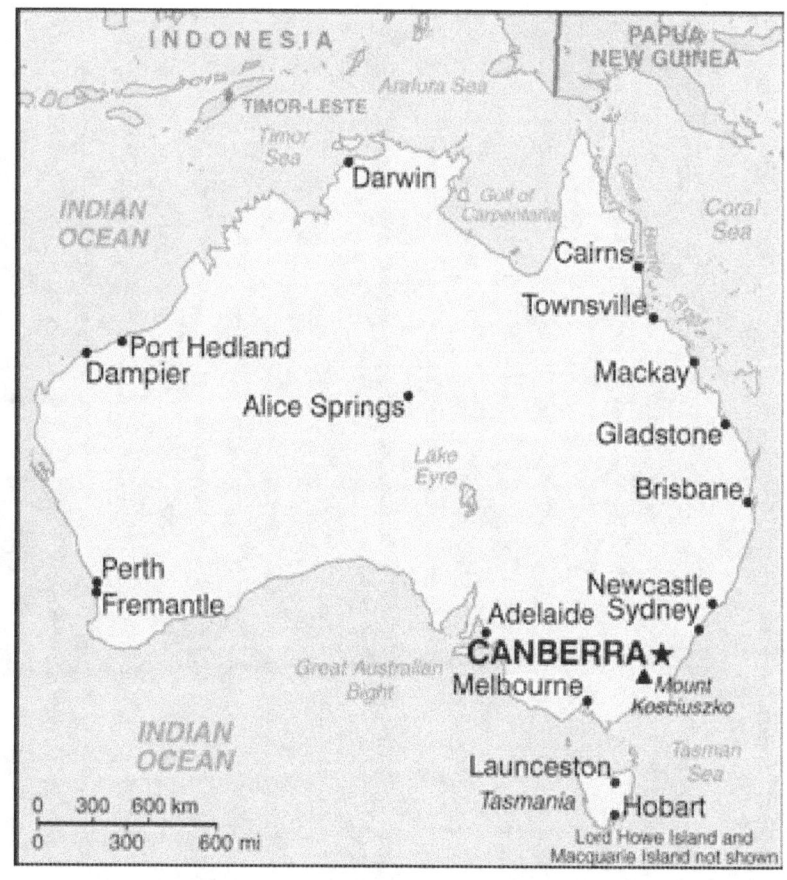

Other Key Facts™ Titles

Key Facts on Syria

Key Facts on China

Key Facts on Qatar

Key Facts on India

Key Facts on Germany

Key Facts on Argentina

Key Facts on Russia

Key Facts on North Korea

Key Facts on Brazil

Key Facts on Italy

Key Facts on the United Arab Emirates

Key Facts on the European Union

Key Facts on Pakistan

Key Facts on Saudi Arabia

Key Facts on Cyprus

Key Facts on Iran

Key Facts on Afghanistan

Key Facts on Iraq

Key Facts on Indonesia

Key Facts on South Korea

Key Facts on France

Key Facts on the United Kingdom

Key Facts on Egypt

Key Facts on Israel

Key Facts on Mexico

Key Facts on the United States of
America

Key Facts on Turkey

Key Facts on South Africa

Key Facts on Greece

Key Facts on Japan

Key Facts on Malaysia

Key Facts on Vietnam

Key Facts on Hong Kong

Key Facts on Jordan

THE INTERNATIONALIST®

2013

WWW.INTERNATIONALIST.COM